For my sister Lacee.

When no one else was there, you were.

I love you.

CONTENTS

You've never met pain like me,

I'll cut you deep.

And stitch you up,

With the fiber of your own morality.

BRITTNEY AKERSON

Poets leave sacrificial pieces of their most vulnerable thoughts on paper with hopes that someone reads them and never has to feel as alone as they have in their lives.

We are not alone.

Ever.

THIS IS US

We work so fucking hard to hide behind the safety of our own terroristic words. In the end we peek at our feet, picking up what is left of our dignity. Revenge, leading to regression. Hatred pursues like the bold bitch she is. An invasion, intruders in black. They don't even conceal themselves anymore, we've fed them like stray cats and now they won't fucking leave. Their home is where my heart used to be, eviction looming. Resistant tenants, sustaining off the crumbs left of me. What's left of you? Do we do this to each other? Are my invaders, in fact, you? Yours, mine?

Can we stop?

b. akerson

TO SHOW YOU VIOLENCE

She lays her head in the curvature of your back. Her merciful mind belongs in the valleys of you.
Her soul though.
Her vigilant and cautionary soul.
Influences the hesitant arch in her back, drags the cage of rib bones around her heart to safety with an abyssal breath. Arms begin shaping barricades between the small of your back and her soul sheltering abdomen.
Forbidding communion.
We fucking know what happens when they fuse. Igniting an inferno of love, anguish, allegiance, and rage. Her soul has grappled with that hell before, veiled in the tsunami of liquor and scar tissue. Still inebriated from the last 'let's work it out'.
Addicted.
She will always want just. one. more. drink. of. you.
Rehab for unhinged, mutilated hearts warranted.
Detox.
Break her down without breaking her. Love her without loving her.
God damnit, make that make sense.

Her soul wants safety not sanity. Match her lunacy.
Rip her wide open and devour her violence.

Before it devours you.

b. akerson

POP. SIP. SWALLOW. REPEAT.

Anguish occupied her eyes.
She's been dismantled,
Reconstructed to appear civilized.

Diagnosed, medicated and absent.
Pop. Sip. Swallow. Repeat.
Suppress memories that leave her rampant.

Winged shadows lurk in her soul.
They cower at the power of the dose,
With it they surrender all control.

Vile screams solicit her logic,
Audacious emotional terrorists.
The taste of disorder leaving them nostalgic.

She nourishes the creatures with heinous ideation,
But only when the dose subsides.
They satisfy prescription damnation.

Pop. Sip. Swallow. Repeat.
Shadows and chaos retreat.

b. akerson

FEEL ME.

Tragedy.

Torture.

You must first feel them.

Rapture.

b. akerson

FOR YOU

The words that flow so freely from her pen,
Never find their way out of her mouth.
Those words, boundless.
Lodged in her throat.
She chokes on each letter,
Killing her at a slow pace.
She's fought, cut and bled for words.
All of them.
She'd fucking rip her own throat out,
Just to hand them to you.
Covered in flesh and blood.
Senseless and hollow.
Futile.
She knew it.
But she'd rather die trying to spit them out,
Then ever try to swallow them again.

b. akerson

NOT ABOUT A BOY

Breathing is a must,
But with you I'm inhaling dust.

Choking, coughing, gagging on you.
While you sit back, smirking as I turn blue.

Your words, a knife piercing my skin.
Blood cascades out from within.

Letting war fall from your tongue,
Not concerned with casualties as long as you've won.

As the sun sets, my emotions rise.
Tears flow, so begins my demise.

My decaying heart no longer beats.
I bow to you.
Take my defeat.

b. akerson

PROMISES

We were looking, just not sure for what. Ourselves? Sanity? Anything that would get us through another night. A distraction of sorts. We stumbled across each other with our literal fingertips, you, my type. Reckless and cynical, a shot of barrel aged whiskey with no chaser. Someone I have to crack, like a code, to reach the depths that interest me. I always found beauty in peeling back the layers of someone's vulnerability. I want to see the pain, the ugly, the damning truth. You do too. I can feel it when I share a room with you, as real as feeling your lips meet my forehead the mornings we share tangled up in your bed. You fucking scare me, and I scare you too. It is a rush of wanting to dive in yet wanting to proceed with extreme caution. Before we penetrated each other's worlds, we made similar promises to ourselves. Never again. Never again, would we allow our hearts to be held by another pair of clumsy hands. Never again would we fall victim to the complete insanity it requires to deconstruct the walls we sacrificed so much to build up. Our safe havens. Never again. It's a suicide mission, yet I want to strap you to my body like the explosive I know you are and risk it all.
b.akerson

31.

Find the beauty in his broken.

Put it on display.

    b. akerson

WAR.

Decay covered in dust.
My heart.
Augmented walls, impassable and towering gates.
I pledged to never unlock them again.
But you, damn you.
A wrecking ball clothed in cologne and a determined grin.
Walls plummet. Gently I die.
Fragmented. Disjointed.
But wait....
My cold heart does not reside alone behind those bricks, cemented with every last drop of purity left in me.
Beasts dwell abaft those gates and bloodied bricks.
If the quest is retrieval of my black heart.
Arrange for war.

b. akerson

WHISKEY WORDS

Throats on fire,
Those words burned on the way out.
Leaving lungs barren,
And hearts brimming with doubt.

b. akerson

INVITATION.

Entice my violence.
Lure my rage.
Encourage my envy.
Revive my pain.
Surface my tears.
Bury my light.
Slaughter my peace.
And then kiss me goodnight.

b. akerson

WORDY WARRIORS

21

A wall?
I've built a fortress.
Armed guards disguised as words.
Lashing out.

Only to keep you from getting in.

b. akerson

ABOUT THE AUTHOR

Brittney Akerson

Brittney has been writing poetry since she was able to pick up a pencil and form complete sentences. She has used writing as an outlet and coping mechanism for many years. Brittney is a mental health advocate and is raising four boys, Calin, Marek, Kai and Riyah, to also be warriors for mental health awareness. Growing up her parents lived in separate states so she traveled between Omaha, NE and Ellsworth, MI every year. Michigan is her favorite "home" and she hopes to one day write a series of poetry books while sipping a glass of wine, on her back porch, overlooking Lake Michigan.

www.ingramcontent.com/pod-product-compliance
Lightning Source LLC
Chambersburg PA
CBHW031257130726
47988CB00008B/3397

THE WOMAN WHO TOUCHED THE SUN

DANIEL RIRDAN

Corino Press

Corino Press
Printed in the United States of America
First Edition(1.0): June 2026

ISBN 979-8-9926090-7-3 (hardcover)
ISBN 979-8-9947039-2-2 (trade paperback)
ISBN v979-8-9947039-5-3 (audiobook)

art by Gennadi Erkulis

Subjects: LCSH:
Interplanetary voyages.
Voyages, Imaginary.
Space flight.
Space vehicles.
Space ships.
Women adventurers.
Blue collar workers.
Sun—Discovery and exploration.
Prometheus (Greek deity)—In literature.

Genre: LCGFT:
Mythological fiction. Fables. Science fiction. Fiction.

Classification:
LCC: PS3618.I68 W66 2026
DDC 813/.6—dc23

*For Gil, and the mechanical spaceship
we designed when we were kids*

It happened in the middle of the night.

Nobody saw her leave. The chickens dozed in their roosts. The farming community lay quiet. The sun was beyond the horizon. Only the stars noticed the barn roof roll open, but they were too far to do anything about it.

She slammed the ignition bar home, and the powerful engines thrummed, sputtered, then roared to life.

The spaceship of blackened iron, pitted brass, and hammered rivets rose up, then burst from the top of the barn. In plumes of blue flame and waves of glassy heat, it flew straight up, tearing through the thick layer of air.

For months she'd worked with a sledgehammer and a welding torch. Each day, she had toiled on the ship after supper, long into the small hours of the morning, until the barn smelled of hot metal and oil.

And now she flew it into space.

The engines rumbled, and the vessel blazed past the wispy clouds. Another long thrust, and the craft broke free of Earth's air and sound—hurtling into the stardust of outer space.

She was going to the sun.

Because.

Her name was Jo.

She had long black hair lashed back without fuss. Strength was written in her posture and the steadiness of her hands. She was the kind of person who made you think twice before interrupting. Who fixed your fence without asking. Who showed up when you were sad.

Some said that long ago she went by the name Kana Yamata—before Nebraska, before the farming community, before the barn.

The cockpit pressed close—copper pipes, tilted walls, a scatter of levers, a cluster of dials—a cramped box, no more than a foot and a half on any side.

Jo wore dark quilted leather, oil-cured, stitched for fire and water and brute work. It wrapped around her in a pattern older than Nebraska. She sat in an elevated tractor-bucket seat. Legs tucked beneath her at rest. Legs down through the gaps when needed: to work the pedals—forward to fly, backward to slow.

All around her, coolant water rose to her chest. It held her in a steadying, heavy embrace that softened the brutal lurch of launch and any sudden bone-deep jolts.

The moon's gravity well tugged at her craft like a hand grabbing an ankle. She pulled the port ballast lever, and coolant water rushed into the compartment on that side, filling it. The ship responded to the shifted weight, leaned into the tug, and skimmed along the moon's edge like a skiff riding a riverbank.

Below her, the moon lay colorless. Gray mountains rose sharp as broken teeth. Bone-white valleys spread like dried riverbeds. Then the great bull's-eye of Mare Orientale rolled beneath the porthole—massive rings of stone rippling outward for hundreds of miles from an ancient wound.

And as the ship streaked over the moon's pock-marked face, something old and cold brushed her mind. But Jo did not answer the startled cry of the moon. She kept silent.

Jo checked the bronze chronometer strapped to the wall—a WWII relic, scarred but faithful. One hour, fifty-three minutes since launch. Next, she studied the moon's bearing. Together, those two numbers gave her what she needed to set course and strike out for the sun.

She twisted in her bucket seat and pulled down to her lap a wooden board—a cut-down barn door. Waxed butcher paper clipped to it.

With a grease pencil dangling from a string, she drew arcs. Marked vectors. Crossed out old numbers. Consulted her waterproof logbook. She grabbed the slide rule and ran the scales—slide, click, slide, calculating. The math was not pretty. It did not need to be. It only needed to be right.

At long last, Jo set and locked a heading, getting the ship under way.

A few minutes in, the gravitational current she was riding began to veer away from the moon—just as the star chart indicated.

The moon's gravity whispered at her heels. The sun's pull pressed on her bow. She threaded the ship between them.

Hour by hour, her ship sped on, and the sun grew—coin to plate to everything. The forward-facing portholes went from dark windows to blazing altars. And a small sound escaped Jo.

The first thermal front hit like a tide. The hull shuddered under the gale of the solar wind: sun-weather, brutal and indifferent. The water heaved. Heat rolled across the hull.

Pedaling, Jo eased the crescent steering wheel over, just enough to bring the reinforced face of the hull into the heat head-on. She rode the thermal front like a wave, letting it push her, carry her closer. Pressure gathered behind her eyes—as if something ahead had noticed her.

Then—

A single hard bang rang through the frame, metal on metal, close and violent. That sounded like trouble.

Jo hauled on the hickory crescent wheel—pitch forward, twist to the side—feeling the hull's flat faces groan as they resisted the gravity stream. She snapped two vents shut. Coolant surged to starboard, and the ship slung itself off course.

She let the craft drift, searching. Somewhere out here, a gravity stream ran toward Mercury—a side current, thin and easy to miss. Jo held her breath as she felt for it the way you would feel for a pulse.

There. A faint tug. She sensed it a moment before the gauges caught up. Jo eased her hold and let the current take her.

The detour was not in the plan. But she had to

find out if the ship had taken damage.

The sun vanished behind Mercury's dark side as the craft slipped into the planet's shadow—plunging the cockpit into midnight in a barrel. It took a few minutes before the glare bled from her eyes, and cold slowly quenched the hot hull. Real cold, offering a blessed relief as it seeped in.

In the dim space, she struck a match. It snuffed out in the draft. She struck another, cupping it, and lit the kerosene lamp. The wick caught with a low whisper. Amber light filled the small cabin and edged back the dark.

She pulled the periscope down from the ceiling to eye level. With both hands on the side handles, she leaned in and looked out through it.

The hull was built to burn away layer by layer, shedding heat with every plate that broke off. Through the scope, Jo saw the sacrificial plates glowing yellow-hot, some already peeled away as intended. She grimaced. One plate must have torn loose wrong and slammed into the hull—that had to be the bang she'd heard. She inspected the outside wall some more. No damage that she could see.

Jo drained the water in the cockpit down to her ankles and unbuttoned her work suit. She opened the small cabinet overhead, took out a jar, pulled free a strip of jerky. Then bit down. The sound of her own chewing felt strange after hours of engine drone. She drank from a thermos and made a face.

Jo was buttoning up when she heard it—a hiss. Faint. Wrong. A sound that hadn't been there before.

She cracked open a wooden service panel and hung the lamp inside the narrow shaft. She looked in and cursed softly. The shock of the earlier impact must have traveled through the metal bones of the ship and found a weak point: a coolant pipe right where it bent. Coolant was now leaking into the duct.

After grabbing tools from the rack above, she pulled herself into the shaft and belly-crawled until she reached the cracked pipe segment.

In the wavering light of a single flame, she loosened the nut. Then let out a low exhale through her teeth as a jet of water sprayed out and snuffed the flame, plunging the shaft into black.

No time to re-light.

By feel, she rammed a spare segment into place and tightened the nut around it. When the wrench finally refused to turn, she backed out of the duct, dripping water and breathing hard.

That would do it. No more leaks.

But coolant had already pooled in the shaft, throwing the vessel off-balance. Pumping it back to storage would cost time—and fuel she didn't have. She'd have to fly the craft as it was, like a sailor steering with a flooded bow.

Jo climbed back into the bucket seat. Intently, she studied the star chart tacked to one of the walls, tracing her current position with her finger. Gravity in this region folded and twisted. A flight trajectory even a hair off, and she'd be dragged sideways, burned broadside.

Finally, she nodded to herself and set the ship on its new heading.

As the engines powered back up to full strength, Jo took a breath and started pedaling. Protective coolant water was refilling the cockpit.

The moment the ship slid out of Mercury's shadow, the portholes detonated into white fire—almost intolerable even while wearing her welding goggles. The metal ribs of the cockpit shimmered. The water burst into sheets of blinding brightness.

Time mattered now.

Jo reached for the control board and brought down a knob wrapped in winter-blue friction tape. The auxiliary refrigeration kicked in with a loud buzz. Coolant channels pumped water like blood through

veins, carrying the sun's fire away from the bones of the ship. Armor.

And as the vessel approached the sun, the temperature needle held steady.

Steady.

Steady.

But then it began to climb. And Jo's eyes widened. Her mouth moved, but no sound came from her parched lips.

Suddenly—pressure. A million thunderstorms in her skull.

"Who dares come so near me?" The roar blasted through her mind.

Sweat now beaded her face. She kept pedaling. Churning through the coolant, every stroke was like pushing a plow through wet clay.

"I forbid!"

Impossible brightness flooded in from all the portholes as the craft drew near the ocean of fire that was the sun. Over her dark-graphite goggles, she slid on furnace glass—inch-thick, black as pitch.

The chronometer ticked steadily on the wall. She counted with it as the ship descended toward the sun's surface. Her jaw was set. Ten minutes. If the craft held together for ten minutes on this heading, she would reach the depth she needed.

Lower and lower. Lower and lower. Lower and lower.
Then—

That was it. She was within reach.

Jo had to move fast now. Every passing second, the inferno was burning through another layer of the outer walls of her spaceship—like flesh from bone.

She hooked her heel on the iron bar and drove it home. The latch snapped free. She heard the deep clang of released metal. Through the outside hatch, the bell went down first—church bronze, repurposed, cracked and heavy, lined with magnetic ore and stubbornness. Trailing after it, a railroad chain snaked out, stamped Burlington, 1887, each link thick as her wrist.

Clank.

Clank.

Clank.

Jo counted by ear. Every tenth link was notched to ring against the hatch. *Clank. Clank. Clank . . . Ping. Clank. Clank. Clank . . . Ping.*

Through half-lidded eyes, she glimpsed the chain vanish into the furnace-white below—before the sight forced her eyes shut.

Steam tore from the vent ports. Every gallon that boiled away bought her seconds—and stole them from the journey home.

Finally: the fifty mark.

She dropped the pin, and the chain went taut, while the inverted bell dipped and scooped.

"You dare?!" roared the sun.

"Yes," Jo said. "I dare."

The sun's pull surged. The cockpit lurched. The water slapped her like a living thing. Her knee banged the pedal frame. Her back slammed into the seat.

Jo lunged forward and seized the windlass spokes. She began to haul up the bell, now thick with liquid sun.

The coolant in the cabin resisted her. The ship groaned. Steam boiled around her.

She hauled anyway. She planted her feet, braced her legs, leaned back—and threw her weight into the spokes. The windlass fought her, and each rotation cost her. The chain outside clanked up, link by link, glowing darker, then brighter, as if flickering between being metal and fire.

The sun shrieked in rage without letup. Fire erupted everywhere. Everything was light.

Slowly, painfully, the church bell rose—yard after yard—liquid sun sloshing against its walls.

The ship was shaking. Everything was shaking.

The water around her was searing hot. The air through her nostrils was scorching steam. Every movement, every breath—torture.

Just then, a lever behind her—one of the coolant trims—jammed. Almost immediately, she felt the heat creeping up. She smelled hot metal, sharper now.

Jo twisted and reached back and pulled on the lever until her forearms shook. The lever grated then screeched then finally righted, metal teeth biting into the ratchet. The buzzing refrigeration deepened again.

Jo turned to the spoked crank and resumed hauling.

And...

And...

And done. The bell slid into its alcove. A small hatch slammed shut behind it.

"Nooooooo!" shrieked the sun in her skull. And it pulled on the ship with a force that would've crushed Jo if not for the water enveloping her.

Jo braced her back against the seat and pushed a foot plate with everything she had, like forcing shut a gate in a storm. "Take us away! Now! Now!" she rasped.

The ship responded with a roar as emergency ballast vents opened, dumping steam and boiling water in a last, desperate attempt to claw free. At the same instant, powerful twin engines—dormant until now, built to burn themselves out over one mighty push— awakened and strained against the terrible gravity of the sun.

The whole frame shook.

For a long moment, the ship hung between forces. Every engine she had roared in one all-out thrust. The sun pulled the other way.

Crrrakks.

The joints screamed.

Crrrakks.

Then—

A slip, a movement.

Another.

And another.

"All things fall to me!" roared the sun.

Jo said nothing, eyes tearing and squeezed shut, breathing the scorching air in ragged gulps. Deep in her throat, she hummed to herself—a hymn her grandmother used to sing in Japan. The same one Jo had sung while churning butter, while storms rolled over the prairie.

Jo had done everything she could.

She lowered herself to the floor.

Who was winning—her engines or the sun? Was she moving away or being dragged back in? She couldn't tell. Around her, above her, below her, everything was an ocean of fire.

Jo sat on the wooden planks, cross-legged. Her

14

back was straight, a black band with white characters tied around her forehead. She forced her eyes open. Her hands trembled. Her gaze held. If she were being drawn toward the sun, she would be consumed soon. Her great-grandfather had been a samurai; he had known how to look death in the eye. She would do no less.

One second passed.
  Another.
  And another.
  Was it. . .?
  Was the burn in her lungs easing—just a little?
  A few more seconds passed.
  Her breathing came easier.
  She let out a shuddering breath. "I did it," she whispered.
  "I did it."

More time passed, and Jo dared a glimpse. The sun was still there—a vast furnace. But now, around its rim, she saw blackness. Space.
  There was no doubt now. She was flying homeward. Back to Earth.
  And she was bringing back a golden liquid she'd taken from the sun.

"Who are you?" came the sun's fading cry from afar.

"My name is Jo," she answered. "Jo from Nebraska."

With shaking hands, Jo removed the dark goggles.

She flew to the sun because. And that was enough.

And there was something else. But Jo never spoke of a thing until it was done.

Ten hours later, she saw Earth—streaked with rich hues of brown, blue, and green, and swirls of white.

Jo was coming home.

Daniel Rirdan wrote *Interstellar Crew* longhand at thirteen, becoming Israel's youngest published novelist. At fifteen, he wrote a book on education reform, hammering away on a rented mechanical typewriter in a laundry closet barely large enough to hold a folding table and a chair.

After military service, he moved to Australia, mastering English with jotted vocabulary lists carried everywhere from the bathroom to tram stops. A year later, the peer-reviewed journal *Foundation* featured his essay on William Gibson.

Decades of detours, dead ends, and one environmental tome later, he returned to speculative fiction at fifty and hasn't looked back since.

From his home in the American Southwest, he writes stories driven by wonder and with no patience for literary fashion. As he sees it, what is possible—or can be imagined—is a wide-open country.

www.danielrirdan.com